CLEVER BACKBONE

JOHN AGARD

Clever
Backbone

BLOODAXE BOOKS

Copyright © John Agard

ISBN: 978 1 85224 822

First published 2009 by
Bloodaxe Books Ltd,
Highgreen,
Tarset,
Northumberland NE48 1

www.bloodaxebooks.com
For further information about Bloodaxe titles
please visit our website or write to
the above address for a catalogue.

Bloodaxe Books Ltd acknowledges
the financial assistance of
Arts Council England, North East.

Cover design: Neil Astley & Pamela Robertson-Pearce.

Printed in Great Britain by
Bell & Bain Limited, Glasgow, Scotland.

For Grace

*Thanks to Charles Darwin for his primate consideration
and to Satoshi Kitamura for the fore-cover
and hind-cover illustrations.*

Yesterday... I strolled a little beyond the glade for an hour and a half... At last I feel asleep on the grass, and awoke with a chorus of birds singing around me, and squirrels running up the trees, and some woodpeckers laughing, and it was as pleasant and rural a scene as ever I saw, and I did not care one penny how any of the beasts or birds had been formed.

Charles Darwin writing from Moor Park to his wife Emma, 1858

1

That farewell to hindlegs that could grasp
a tree-top's cradle. Clutch fruit. Crack a nut.
Now the looking into a mirror of grass
with those herds given to aeons grazing.

Auroch. Gazelle. Antelope. That earthbound lot
hoofed and honed for open plain all-fours lifespan.
But nostalgia for tree-swinging would bring
root and bulb no closer. Whereto grassland?

Ah, this vertical sunrise of buttocks
this angling of thighbone towards savanna
this freedom of forelimbs to shape and pluck.

And yet, an upright surge into who-knows-what?

So wish them both the best of primate luck
He-kind and She-kind toddling towards horizons.

2

Rejoice in the backbone
even if it arrived
a few million years late.

Say Viva Vertebrate
for this vertical boost
to evolution's throne.

Will backbone rule the roost
of the chain of being?
Who thought up this invention?

Without the backbone
you couldn't do the jive
or stand to attention.

Backbone, aren't you clever?
Better late than never.

3

Where are the glyptodonts now
with their club of a tail?
Where are the dinosaurs
with their coat of mail?

Clubbing it in oblivion.
So much for spikes and scales.
Fat lot of good it did
that armoured battalion.

Who cares for skin that's stud-hard
when a boss-brain is hominid's
up-the-sleeve trump card.
So let them keep their carapace.

Here comes human race.
Just you watch this space.

4

Step gently, furry friend, on that upright ladder.
The higher the stepper, the higher the tumble.
But don't let that put a spoke in evolution's wheel.
There's time yet to develop an Achilles heel.
Hang loose a while in this almost-human stage.
Go with the flow before the hang-ups and the rage.

Not quite Homo. Getting there. Still Hominid.
Not yet conscious of Freud and all his id.
Bipedal, yes. But still that apeish crouch.
No reason yet for the psychiatric couch.
All the cosmos you crave is in a berry.
So evolve slowly towards the chair of therapy.

Furry friend, hand-on-chin, the way Rodin's thinker thinks.
So almost-human. So without need for a shrink.

5

Unburdened. No property as yet to pass on.
Unless a branch could be called inheritance.
At least you'll leave a family resemblance
to more than a few thousand generations.
Even in those of so-called blue-blood lineage,
one can spot that splitting simian image.

Possessions? Not much. Mainly miscellaneous
termite-teasing twigs and stones for cracking nuts.
Maybe a few footprints bridging continents.
But really no need for last will and testament.
Your legacy? – an upright stride to icy Europe.
But O the shiver in the bones. How did you cope?

Nothing like a steady fire, a good old story
and unsigned cave paintings for posterity.

6

Witness a palette steeped in nature's clay
deep in caves far off daylight's beaten track.
Ah, to see an antlered beast at prowl and play
across an unframed stretch of treeless rock.

For though stalactites ticked to their Ice Age clock
there was warmth in earth's bounty of colour.
From ground-up-bones, look, a silhouette of chalk
and heaven's blood comes hidden in ochre.

One day, among glass galleries of arty talk,
will you take for granted that first revelation
of a horse's head released from a charcoal stump
or how fingertips brushed a bison into motion?

You had no word for private view or acrylic
but old gods reviewed your burnt wood magic.

7

Now, now, not so fast, Woman Erectus.
Getting this – shall we say – pee-posture correct
is a necessary bottom-line must.
This is no time for you to pirouette.

You must try to master the hang of the squat.
Remember, you're not a bursting Wood Stork
in some uninhibited habitat.
And long may you flow like champagne uncorked.

As for you, Man Erectus, try to maintain
a stand-up state when bladder begins to rain.
You must come to grips with words like *Ladies*, *Gents*
and of course last but not least *Incontinents*.

One day toilet thrones shall be an invention
And unraised seats a bone of contention.

8

Her bottom may have lost its baboon-blush
and the tail that talent to swing and clutch.
Gone all those arboreal naps quietly snatched
in the forked cradle of a branch

Now water's diamond dimensions test the spine
something in her wants to weep like a seal
till tears mingle with the salt of ocean.
Don't millennia pass quickly when you're having fun?

Now horsing waves come to take her for a ride
and she would gladly be a dolphin's bride
if only scrub land would release her heel
O to be an amphibian, blessed with two dominions

And walk arm in arm with sea and with land.
Like taking the coming of love with both hands.

9

How does a tiny filament of bone
tune itself to water's dense microphone?
How does a gill prepare to become a jaw
and a jaw graduate to middle ear?
Do reptiles hold the key to this jigsaw
of bone plucking music from the spheres?

Why lose sleep over such miracles? The higher
you climb that brittle vertebrate ladder,
the more your gains and losses synchronise.
Gone are the acoustricks of your swim bladder,
and once lungs were the perfect amplifier
of secrets shared between ocean and sky.

Now, you must put your ear to the future
and trust in your eardrum's inner fanfare.

10

Back in the forest, fruits beckoned She-kind's tastebuds.
How would she cope with life in the grassland hood?

A diet of grasshoppers simply won't do
not when you're a pregnant primate eating for two

A tree-dweller's got to prove her grassland-cred
or end up a sucker to some quadruped.

Better to chill out with those turtles in the sea
than rub shoulders with a canine-toothed posse.

So off to the water's edge for a scuttling snack
for crabs haven't yet tweaked that pebbles break the back.

But looks like a bipedal is after her behind
pushing his way up the anthropoid line.

No need to prove She-kind's a pebble-proud tool-shaper.
Just stay cool in her new sub-cutaneous layer.

11

An articulate ape on a two-legged throne
lording it over creeping flesh and bone?
Is this how you picture yourself in time's frame?

Sovereign of beast of earth and fowl of air
ensconced on your self-appointed apex
yet subject to the smallest flying insects.

Damn those mosquitoes with their spitfire stings
and that fly of diminutive grey matter
that manages to outwit your fly-swatter

If naming grants dominion over tooth and claw
at least hang on to your sense of awe.
Still cower if you can at the thunder's note

and the blood flow tuned to the moon and the tides.
Wonder at She-kind's monthly eclipse of the thighs.

12

She who comes to suckle your sleep with night's cauldron
of moon-brewed tidings.

She who comes to lift the weight of your sunlit cares
and wrap you in the void's first garment.

She who comes to gather your days in her dark genesis
and shield you from logic's blinding enlightenment.

She who comes to teach you the art of silent flowering
and replenish with the black gesture of seed becoming
flesh and blood birthright.

What will you make of a mothering darkness
but a mirror for the heart's demons.

A primal reason for crimes committed
in the name of light –

Already the Inquisition is putting on its hood.

13

This red elixir of a waterfall
over rock of bone. Let's agree to call
it Blood. Yes, Blood. One syllable will do
for that river that runs in the veins of all
and washes over tradition and taboo.

They say the first drop spilled was all it took
to begin the first rose that can pierce thornwise
and seize the heart by passion's hook and crook.
Blood that crowns the sorrow of paradise
and scatters its petals of forgiveness.

See how it leaves its print on history's purest page.
This moon-blessed companion of life and death.
This wine that clings to a common vine of flesh.
See how it stains your cloth of joy as well as rage.

14

No time like the present to think of Armageddon.
But for now just enjoy being a two-legged one.
Concentrate on mastering the bipedal style.
You've got millennia to perfect a missile.

Grassland horizons are waiting to be solved.
So why not save freed-up hands for better things
like scratching and caress of swimming haunches.
Before you know it, you would have evolved
to modern hominids with beer-brimming paunches.

Remember, O you kind without fins or wings,
a backbone isn't all it's cracked up to be.
A backbone has its drawbacks. Upright posture
its downside. So don't start acting uppity.

Slipped discs and backache are already your future.

15

Fire's gift. Cave walls a ripple of shadows.
Breath-blown stars as comforting as a host
of fireflies – a traveller's flickering map.
As good a time as any to forage in a lap.

Time to enjoy certain bipedal perks.
Surrender the body to full-frontal quirks.
Make the most of two mouths joined plum to plum.
Ah. This rubbing of cranium on cranium.

Consider it, if you wish, as heaven-sent –
this face-to-face lying of length to length.
Yes, this clinch of eyes and whisper while you mount
is a blessing Homo will one day learn to count.

But will backbone receive a curse or compliment
when belly on belly rejoices fully spent?

16

And Woman Erectus who shall be childblessed
shall have to endure a harrowing test –
For when the moment has come to deliver
She-kind might wish her pelvic bowl was bigger.

As for you, stride-strutting Erectus Homo,
self-absorbed in vertical progressing,
you won't escape this mixed bipedal blessing
for your lower back shall cry lumbago.

And would you think your kind smart-ass superior
when prone to the harass of a hernia?
But the up side outweights the down side.
Knuckle-walking apes won't manage your stride

And your hands shall extend into javelins.
And be free to travel the frontiers of skin.

17

What of skin, your ephemeral cling-film
that keeps the inside on its shelf of bones?
Whether body type be fat, thin or middling,
without skin your skeleton's stranded. On its own.
All skin by the way must pass its sell-by date.
Even the skin of a civilised primate.

What of skin, your well-weathered birthright parchment
that was meant for the wind's caressing feather
Or for a lovestruck finger to trace galaxies
where time keeps no record of lesser and better.
Skin, the hairy Eden of grooming Chimpanzee
Skin, the hairless paradise of romping Otter.

And yet Homo Sapiens will make laws to resist
this letting go of epidermis to epidermis.

18

And what rules will your evolving face follow?
Is the face with the pleasing perfect ratio
a Renaissance cherub by a Bellini
or a countenance of Oriental slant?

Is width of mouth to cheekbone at the right cant
for the contours of an Aborigine
Or must you look for model symmetry
in the profile of a Nefertiti?

Who can solve the human face? What a puzzle.
Not straightforward as a four-footer's muzzle.
What you see is what you get. Straight to camera.
No creed. No race. No beauty formula.

Better perhaps the fate of the sea-urchin –
greeting passing strangers as faceless kin.

19

So what's it to be, smiling Homo Erectus?
Would you rather be a tooth-walking walrus
or does the beaver's ready sharpened chisel
put your own incisors to blunt shame? Ah, well.

Never mind. You'll learn how a morsel of love-bite
can satisfy another kind of hunger.
So be it. He-kind. She-kind. Feast on each other.

Why pine for a baboon's larger canine
when you can flash a row of pearly whites
and convince yourselves that to chew is divine.
Already your molars are growing into a grin.

So let the unsung task of teeth begin.
Those teeth you bare to keep an enemy at bay
will outlive flesh in the face of death's decay.

20

Hello white Erectus
Bet you've been taken aback
to discover your family tree
begins with an African black –
a foxy fossil lady named Lucy.

Not Lucy in the sky with diamonds
Lucy in the earth with skeletons.

People get ready evolution's train a–coming.
People get ready evolution's train a–coming.
Got a ticket all the way to Savanna.
Gonna find you a black bipedal Momma.

Archaeologist, hop on the bandwaggon
'cause Lucy sure can rattle that pelvic bone
out of reach of Dr Presumed Livingstone.

21

So much for those pedestals of purity
when Africa bears Europe's genetic tree.
And you can't catch genes just talking on the phone.
You got to engage with the flesh and the bone.

Is it coffee in the milk or milk in the coffee
that puts the degree in your pedigree?
Is it a case of boundaries growing into home
or wherever you lay your genes that's your genome?

While civilisations hype their myths of glory,
under the sheets history tells its under-story.
A word in the ear can lead to primeval kissing.
Before you know it, your buttocks are twitching.

Looks like purity has lost its street-cred
when gardens everywhere flaunt their hybrids.

22

You can't have it both ways. Or as you'll say
when your tongue discovers idioms –
You can't have your cake and eat it. Unhindered play
of arms has its hidden fine-print conditions.

Foot can no longer be guaranteed to grasp.
No chance of reimbursement for loss of branch.
Monkey-toes henceforth handle nut-breaking tasks.
But for Homo that would be too much to ask.

So save hands for bark plus bark equals spark.
Save hands for fire-making in the dark.
Save hands for shadow-stories on cave walls
before telly comes to colonise your eyeballs.

Simply say ta-ta to all-fours posture.
Hello to epiphany of gesture.

23

Hands that must learn to grope and grapple
are half-way to designing the Sistine Chapel.
But bet that marble-wizard Michelangelo
forgot he was once a hand-fumbling Homo.
And hands that fashioned Benin's bronze kingdom
began with mastering the rebel thumb.

Hands that once fumbled in a manual mist
will applaud an Houdini-style escape artist.
And hands that adapt to arrow and bow
might well evolve to the concert hall cello.
Woodchipping is not a bad place to start.
Not bad for an upcoming upright upstart.

Yet hands can have an ulterior mission –
reducing other hands to submission.

24

See Homo Habilis
and Mrs Habilis
and little Habilis in tow.

It's not off to the Wizard of Oz
but off to the land of IKEA they go.

Do-it-yourself survivors
self-assembling houseproud gods
and all it takes is a Phillips screwdriver.

Nomads of the flatpacked,
all power to your handy knack.

But who will polytex your polycrags
when the world outside is raining bricks

and the instructions inside
are indecipherable hieroglyphics?

25

Eat your heart out – waltz, foxtrot, paso doble.
You ain't got nothing on the palaeolithic jive
when dancing took the lead from how to survive
and hairy feet danced the stone age blues away.

O those days when dancing meant survival
in motion. The poetry of pantomime.
Keeping the beat grounded in ritual.
How the art of movement and creatures chimed.

How else can that deer come to your beck and call
if you don't become one with antlers and hooves?
How else can that spear return lucky with bear
if you don't enter fur and a grizzly groove?

So shake that antler, baby, strut that thing.
Becoming four legs on two makes magic swing.

26

How does cave man say *Honey I'm home?* Uttered
a footstep away from his rock of welcome
and moving towards a cuddle of bear fur.

And raising from her shaping pot of clay,
how does cave woman ask *Babes, how was your day?*
And the kiddie ponders a puzzle of pebbles –
how from rattle they magic into flame.
Do pebbles, like the heart, cry out for a name?

Don't underestimate the nuances of grunts
when the throat threatens to burst into syllables
and there's a day of bison-tracking to recount.

Time for an early night to try out mouth-sounds –
their ooohs and aaahs joining limbs and lobes.
Blubbering love piercing the wordless bone.

27

She-kind's back from a day at the office
to bring home the bacon in a briefcase
for she has become a working primate mum
foraging the nine-to-five tedium
to keep her young well-groomed for the rat race.

He-kind meanwhile with a new man's vigour
is following with a vacuum cleaner
the spoor of a carpet's dust-ridden trail.
He draws the line at wearing an apron
though he'll wash up more nimble than a gibbon.

Will role reversal reverse domestic strife
when a house-husband replaces a housewife?
Armed with filofax she stalks workaday stress
while he mops up the floor with a caveman's zest.

28

Remember the moment your mouth first danced
to the tune of cooked flesh? It was just by chance –
which is one way of saying the gods fixed it –
that you stumbled on fire's benefits.

Thanks to bark and stone for this burning shield
against the cold and night-time predator.
But who'd have guessed that embers would reveal
how a roasted leg improves its flavour?

So, will He-kind or She-kind get the credit
for discovering this char-grilling moment
when they come to feast on golden chicken
as they strut a designer fitted kitchen?

Ah, at peace on a fire-blushing pillow,
Homo dreams of hard sinew and raw marrow.

29

He-kind sleeps through a dripping tap
while wide-eyed She-kind gets into a flap.

And when He-kind swagger-slumps into bed
there's no pillow to prop the fruit of his head.
But does he mind? No. You'd swear husband Erectus
had a direct line to the ear of Morpheus.

Lucky those sloths that sleep even upside down
And those apes dreaming in tree-tops' eiderdown.
Is insomnia what Woman Erectus gained
from striding upright on an open plain?

Torn between the tap's solo and hubbie's snore
she's tried oils and herbs to dispel the octaves
rising from a throat-orchestrated night-score.
Yet predators once paused before snore-filled caves.

30

Observe the hind parts of the four-footed ones
and give thanks for the bounty of your derrière.
For though fangs and claws are champs at bite and tear
uprightness will bequeath perk to your B-hemisphere.
Consider Homo Sapiens tops of the bottoms.

Lion's head may wear the jungle's crown
but that royal beast doesn't reign superior
when it comes down to the posterior.

True, Chimpanzee can flicker her hindquarter bulbs
and Rabbit frisk his bit of bob as bunnies do.
But Homo Sapiens will lead the rear-view.

Some things you will lose, some things you will gain.
You two-footers will lose your tree-swinging tail
but you'll gain a rear more globular than your brain.

31

When two or more posteriors join their ends,
that's not a bad start to becoming friends.
So get on with it, Homo Sapiens.
Let that jaw drop and O let those eyes gape
though even pair-bonding can go pear-shaped.

Prepare for the coming of pre-nupt arrangements
when love and the law become entertwined
and scales of justice weigh the size of nest-eggs.
Yes, assets shall walk down the aisle with assets
and desire lie down on a dotted line.

Make the most of these days when a marriage licence
means a share in the fire and the bison.
Why bog down your cranium in percentages
when you're getting the hang of appendages.

32

Before a soft word comes to turn away wrath
you would have learnt to present the buttocks
as a peace alternative to the warpath
for a raised rump can keep at bay a rain of rocks.

Alas, this means of forestalling aggression
will be lost on the Geneva Convention –
this long gone protocol of the fundament
will not figure in the First Amendment.

So before your bombers take to the skies
and your round tables square up for hostilities
remember how once your bipedal thighs
were privy to bilateral treaties.

Remember, Homo Sapiens, how once you sat
upon a bottom's unweaponed covenant of fat.

33

And now booty-licious enters the language.
And a red carpet rear makes the front page.

But what would one paraded in Europe's glass
and rebaptised the Hottentot Venus
make of this augmentation of the ass?

One no less Homo, one no less Erectus
than the scientists who would preserve her –
a specimen for curiosity's mirror.

O Hottentot Venus, no Botticelli shell
saw you rise from the void of a London freakshow
though you had your own earth-mother story to tell.

And when Paris made an eye-full of your Otherness
you were more than dark flesh in the Eiffel's shadow.
You were two continents diminished to a gaze.

34

Hear the mating call of the *Lonely Hearts* column –
a primal howl across a page's calm.
In this your search for the elusive Right One,
tick relevant box to confirm criterion.

Do you seek a no-strings primate playmate
or a long-term down-the-aisle candidate?
Are you a mix-and-match bi-bi-bipedal
or a strictly missionary horizontal?

Please take care to answer this questionnaire
stating if you're allergic to body hair.
Mutual grooming cannot be guaranteed
but there's someone out there to match your every need.

A sense of humour of course always helps
so enclose enlarged photo of your cortex.

35

Now it is the season of the leg-over
fireflies flash their come-ons to all comers
and the randy deer out to pull tonight
relies on antlers to rule the spotlight.

See how the fiddler crab rises on tiptoe
to the violin of his libido
and the peacock flaunts his fanfare of eyes
as if to prove God's gift comes in plumage size.

But lady baboons always cut to the chase.
When the fellows are slow at catching her drift
she'd thrust her flaming assets in their face.

O upright Man supine with a cigarette,
spare a thought for that post-coital mantis
saying his last prayer in a lover's abyss.

36

Gladly would you surrender your Chanel
if you could truly yield to an armpit's smell.
And would you rather inhale a packaged Brute
than the brush of sweat perfumed with nature's roots?

When body-signals go dead like your dial tones
will Nose recall the one-to-one of pheromones?
That sudden musk from a forked branch of thigh.
That whiff in the air beyond the grasp of eye.

And if scent is a news-bringer of taste
what fruit is that oozing downwards from the waist?
And how long ago was it since bonding flowered
in the radiant compost of a single odour?

O the loss of smell in on-line dating
especially when She-kind is ovulating.

37

What's with the clothing, Homo? Is it to protect
from weather's wear and tear, not to mention insects,
or is it to adorn your mortal nudity
and spell out loud who's a he and who's a she?

Fur, leather, skin, grass, all have their uses
for keeping limbs in fashionable nooses.
But can a coat, even of finest velvet,
stop the rain from doing its job, which is to wet?

Don't say you've suffered a blow to your morale –
to be born a frail unarmoured mammal?
Nothing like the armadillo or porcupine
with their breastplate and infantry of spines.

How compete with such castle of skin? Ah well,
Let clothes be your armour, your washable shell.

38

That skin of yours shall play host to parasites.
That hair of yours shall be a harbour for mites
and they shall teach you the art of good grooming.
Can you think of a more heart-warming spectacle
than hands foraging among hair follicles
or plucking a louse from a loved one's flesh?

Though you've lost hair in the bipedal process,
amoebae shall make your clothes their residence.
You might not be as hairy as cousin chimpanzee
but that armpit of yours shall be refuge for fleas.
And they shall teach you the art of good grooming
when love signals from the discomfort of an itch.

Have regard for the tiny of earth's dominion.
Treat parasites as your furtive companions.

39

And the seeds of speech shall sprout at your mouth's door.
And the branch of the larynx shall blossom
with the fruit of pitch and volume. Crop of tongues.
So, Homo, peel a sound down to a vowel's core.

Now try the joy of eating a consonant raw
with a little help of course from a lowered jaw,
courtesy of a bipedal spin-off.
Hear how a word can cast an inner spell
and even turn the bone of logic soft.
Hear how a name uttered rings its own bell

But unlike that blade hafted from a deer's antler –
no dug-up fossils of your glimmering grammar.
No carbon dating to fix those fire-long nights
when syllables were munched free of spin and soundbites.

40

No doubt a chimp can come to grips with coded signs.
but not with the *Confessions* of St Augustine.
No, chimps don't read those classics with black august spines.

You won't see a great ape like the Bonobo
appear on a Parkinson primate-time chat-show
though some call an ape's vocals proto-lingo.

On the scale of talk you claim the highest rung.
You – upright Homo with your globe-trotting tongue
and a finger on the trigger of your lexicon.

Parrots merely mimic what they can't read or spell.
But you fancy yourself just below the angels
all because of your consonants and vowels.

If you think hard work was shaping an axe,
you wait till you come to whittle at syntax.

41

O Grass-graze   Moo-chew
Bell-shake   Milk-brew

Is that your own unaided unwritten-down effort
Poet-in-the-making Homo Erectus
or did the Muse provide a push-start?
Not a bad little monosyllabic
praisesong. A touch of the rhapsodic
for a creature you will come to call Cow.
Looks like poetry will sit beside the plough
for Homo is discovering budding iambics.
Let Woman autograph it with the name Anon.
One day it might be part of the Lit. Canon.
Let critics call your style pre-literate
and trace your theme to primate origin.
In the blink of a quill you'll maximise the margin.
Now Homo's well on the way to post-literate.

42

From a single cell to the Tower of Babel.
See what happens when you spoil an angel?

Give these hominids a syllable's bounty
and they start thinking they're a Chomsky.

Given half a chance, this upstart Erectus
will soon be catching up on Catullus.

Today the windfall of a common tongue,
tomorrow a whirlwind threat to sky's dominion.

Any self-respecting bearded patriarch
would put a damper on Homo's linguistic spark.

Confusing their consonants and vowels
may separate the vertebrates from the angels.

Topple earth-bound words that try to be Icarus.
Let Homo see how it feels when speech bites the dust.

43

So how shall you deal with space's domain?
Answer, O Sapiens of frontier-making brain.

Will a chimp's markings begin the birth of maps?
What if habitable space should overlap
into a mixed rubbing of tribal shoulders
and love be not pinned to a land's perimeter?

What if global space prove hard to accommodate?
There are always manned borders if need be.
Perhaps a simple sign that says NO ENTRY.
A spoor of a flag to claim the moon's estate.

And so the common cat sprays urine for its key and latch.
The hamster mortgages a homestead with a scent.
The human applies a lick of paint to its patch,
keeping a guarded eye on a godly fence.

44

Hurray for Homo
now a space-suited Apollo
first-footing the moon's surface
with a giant leap for the human race

Hope of planet Coca-Cola
for a stars and stripes generation
thirsty for gravity.
Roll over super nova.

O flag-planting Erectus
to oblivion's unfathomable scorecard
you have added your astro noughts.

Is that blind Galileo
scanning the dust
for a morsel of star?

45

Where is the beast of tooth and claw that will fast
to see that social injustice breathes its last?
No way Jose. Doctrine-driven hunger-strikes
haven't caught on among fur, feathers and spikes.

Where is the hungry Lion that will not munch
a sitting-duck-of-an-antelope-lunch
because the long-chosen road to liberation
starts under a banner of starvation?

Let praise be rendered where praise is due.
Only omnivorous Homo Erectus would choose
to starve for country, creed or taboo.
Which other creature makes a statement with its stomach?

And yet this self-starving primate paradox
would stone a sinner with retributive rocks.

46

Pondering four-footed facial expressions,
Darwin concludes that orang-utans don't frown.
As for smiling, out of the question.
Not even a toothless twinkle of the gums.
And let's be honest, receding rainforests
aren't exactly something to smile about.
Is it a given then and irrefutable
to say that orang-utans are inscrutable?
No hope of scrawling the canvas of the face
with the doodle of a fleeting grimace?

But take heart, one day across continents
Orang-utans shall interact by internet.
A click of a mouse shall set sparks in motion
and furry gestures give context to a frown.

47

Not the canine's
hangdog excuse for a grin

Not the feline's
creamy Cheshire

Not the terrapin's
beaming jaw-line fixture

or for that matter the crocodile's
toothsome profile.

Be grateful, friend Homo,
for the small divine

mercy of a smile –
the heart's genuine blossom.

Ah, fleeting little rainbow
that jewels the clouds of cheeks.

48

Ah, the sad trumpet of an old elephant
under the gaze of a neutral moon
because his long-term trunk-partner is no more.

Ah, the grief-gutted cry of the bereaved baboon
when the soulful berries of a mate's eyes
finally surrender their light.

Ah, the chest-thumping of a widowed Gorilla
whose nimble grasp cannot get to the root
of why this no-companion day is a joy-killer.

And you, friend Homo, how shall you find comfort
when the broken-heart days come with their void?
Cry brother. Cry sister.

The gift of tears is on your side.
And time a shoulder to lean on.

49

If you should be so lucky as to encounter
a Neanderthal on a crowded street,
make eye-contact. Don't just look at his feet.
Greet him by his mouthful name. He'll be impressed.

Say *Hi Homo Sapiens Neanderthalensis.*
Say Do you know you've had a very bad press?
They've made you into a club-swinging grunter.
A beetle-browed butt of stand-up gags.
A shaggy half-clad ambling towards a shag
long vanished with the bison and the ice sheets.

Stop a while for a one-to-one chin-wag
with this chinless trekker from frozen tundras.
Observe how his grunts and gestures grow familiar.
Shake hands with yourself mirrored in time's timeline mists.

50

Pause a while at that Cro-Magnon cranium
mouldered into the light of a museum.
Difficult to say for sure if the skull's blonde.
A skull as yet unschooled in Aryan *Fatherlond*.

Head axe-blade-scarred and two molars vacant.
A skull that is beginning to be ashamed
to claim someone like Hitler for a descendant.
Yet speaking mammals once uttered his name.

Pause a while at that Cro-Magnon cranium.
How long since it dreamt of spears in a wild hide?
Never in its wildest tree-bred beginnings,
the long slow pilgrimage to genocide.

O for the boundless grasslands grace of the giraffe,
under a far sky unscarred by any Luftwaffe.

51

Remember, branching days long gone, my talking ape,
how your mouth first fostered an *Ah* and *Oh!*
Common expletives revealed their rainbow.
Seeded embryos of words were taking shape
at flinch of cut thumb, at height of pleasure's tide,
at call of hunger from the stomach's cave.
For what is syllable twinned to syllable
by limb of breath if not a miracle,
you now take in your everyday erectus stride?

So grunts evolved into grammar. And from your wardrobe
of slogans – the unpalatable ghosts of Carnage
shall be dressed up as Collateral Damage.
Is this what the gift of speech intended
when words first bloomed beside the tongue's orchid?

52

Standing looking lost among supermarket aisles,
only in your reptilian memory
will you remember foraging days in the wild
when the open plains were your food-pantry?

A slouching skin-pouch was then your trolley.
And rooting among nature's special offers
there were no signs of buy-one-get-one-free –
no Bogof tracks to lead to temptation
when your thoughts were on a tasty crustacean.

Shopping lists then were carved in fleeting thoughts:
How long before that antelope is caught?
Now you are a stalking shopper at the check-out
following the trail of your chocolate-grubbing snout.

Ah, reptilian memory.

53

After centuries adapting to the mobile,
Homo's earlobes shall evolve Mr Spock style.
As mobile phones become the new erogenous zones,
earlobes shall throb to handset titillation –
that is if earlobes survive radiation.
Put it down to long-term effects of mobile-speak.
But earlobe and handset shall quench each other's needs
on the sweating pillow of a cheek.
See earlobes quiver to the caress of a ringtone
and handsets respond with a mind of their own.
Earlobes shall have a new lease on the libido.
And it's pay as you go, Babes, pay as you go.
Prepare for earlobes evolved to fishlike gills
and handsets mutating to blushing thrills.

54

Well well well thesaurus-tongued Homo Erectus,
looks like you've sparked a planetary rumpus.
And if you still insist you're Sapiens
instinctly distinct from four-footed-friends
then dig this. Remember how you monkeyed about,
frog-kicked, piggy-backed, fox-trotted, bear-hugged, bugged
and badgered one another? Silly Cow you'd shout
for a lark. Remember those goosepimples and puppy
loveflutters when you swore you were the bee's knees,
the cat's whiskers? O the hen-night stag-night affairs!
You learnt to talk cold turkey and go the whole hog.
And didn't you join the rat-race and the dog-eat-dog?
With the passing of years you shed crocodile tears
And alas your whale of a time has turned your swansong.

55

Yet when memory's rose
becomes a vase of ash
and the Reaper's wand
cuts short love's sweet aria

Look for rainbows
in tadpole-teeming ponds
where night's spermatozoa
blossom into croaking beauties.

Look for signs
from caterpillar messengers –
those hair-shirted heralds
of Messiah butterflies.

The twinkling gills of a star
Somewhere in your pool of genes.

56

You've come a long way from the primeval soup
when molecules hadn't boiled into racial groups.
You won't recall that moment of mutation.
Look at you now. You've grown into global nations.
Your backbone stands tall to national anthems
that help maintain *Erect Us* from *Erect Them*.

Your vowels have blossomed into pixels
and your hairy fingers evolved to a mouse.
Now you've learnt how to pluck a living cell
and relocate it to a test-tube house.
But you're still a primate, that's the bottom line.
Civilisations still wag their behinds.

But your atrocities have got a good excuse.
Blame the primeval soup that reproduced.

57

See how the wordless ones have served you well.
Look no further than a stone or a shell.
How the dumb stone sprouts a tongue of fire
to warm your soul and bring heart to home.
How the shell curled into its own mute self
becomes in your ear the voice ear of the sea.

See how the wordless ones have served you well.
Cherish that lump of clay and piece of bone.
How the moulded clay becomes articulate
and mothers a dialogue of gourds.
How the bone can speak of past and future
and tease the tongue into a dance of octaves.

Listen to the tongueless ore tuning its iron
for songs of harvest and cries of broken ones.

58

A hunter's bond no longer life insurance.
A forager's quest a backward-looking glance.
And everywhere cities of lights advance.
Cave frescoes receded into the Gothic.
And darkness blinks at the flick of a switch.

Fireflies elsewhere. Now neon time beckons
old homesteads towards migrant ground.
But necropolis precedes metropolis,
so the dead will adapt to all conditions.

See Mesopotamia risen from the Tigris
and the Indus reborn in Mohendro-daro.
And from the backs of humans branded cargo
sprout Lisbon, London, New York, Paris, Madrid.
What a long way you've flown, wingless hominid.

59

You lost your hind legs but you kept your hindsight
which comes in handy when foresight blunders.
Somewhere between the zones of black and white
your reptile brain sheds another skin of truth
and instinct somehow manages to creep under
the house of logic you built on absolutes.

You might have turned your backbone from the trees
but O no, you won't shake off those chimpanzees
still swinging among the branches of your genes.
Note the way you behead a banana,
scratch your parts and groom before a mirror –
making faces at yourself – your Other.

Yet what makes a verbal mammal hesitate
when an endangered reflection gestures soul-mate.

60

Beloved Hominid paradox
is there no stopping your vertical clock,
no backing down to your backbone,
no end to your vertical quest?

And when the final reckoning has come
will you consider your fate cursed or blessed?
If you had to do it all over the next time round
would you opt for a bipedal progress?

Beloved Hominid paradox
will your Hosannas replace your Hiroshimas
or will your self-created disasters
stand in the way of your Happy-Ever-Afters?

Is it too early to start taking stock
or is the writing written in rock?

John **Agard** was born in Guyana and came to Britain in 1977. He has published two collections with Serpent's Tail, *Mangoes and Bullets* and *Lovelines for a Goat-Born Lady*, and five books with Bloodaxe, *From the Devil's Pulpit* (1997), *Weblines* (2000), *We Brits* (2006), *Alternative Anthem: Selected Poems* (2009) and *Clever Backbone* (2009).

He is a popular children's writer whose titles include *Get Back Pimple* (Viking), *Laughter is an Egg* (Puffin), *Grandfather's Old Bruk-a-down Car* (Red Fox), *I Din Do Nuttin* (Red Fox), *Points of View with Professor Peekaboo* (Bodley Head) and *We Animals Would Like a Word with You* (Bodley Head), which won a Smarties Award. *Einstein, The Girl Who Hated Maths*, a collection inspired by mathematics, and *Hello H₂O*, a collection inspired by science, were published by Hodder Children's Books and illustrated by Satoshi Kitamura. *The Young Inferno*, his retelling of Dante, also illustrated by Satoshi Kitamura, was published by Frances Lincoln Children's Books in 2008. His anthology *Hello New* (Orchard Books, 2000) was chosen by the Poetry Society as its Children's Poetry Bookshelf Best Anthology.

His collection, *Half-Caste* (Hodder Children's Books, 2004), includes the poem 'Half-Caste', studied by countless GCSE students and which he has performed with GCSE Poetry Live to thousands across the country.

He collaborated with Bob Cattell on *Butter-Finger* (Frances Lincoln, 2005), a cricket novel for children to which he contributed calypso cricket poems.

He won the Casa de las Américas Prize in 1982 for *Man to Pan*, and in 1997 was one of the five poets given the Paul Hamlyn Award for Poetry. He was also twice winner of the Guyana Prize, for *From the Devil's Pulpit* and *Weblines*. He was shortlisted for the 2007 Decibel Writer of the Year Award for *We Brits*.

As a touring speaker with the Commonwealth Institute, he visited nearly 2000 schools promoting Caribbean culture and poetry, and has performed on television and around the world. In 1989 he was awarded an Arts Council Bursary and in 1993 became the first Writer in Residence at London's South Bank Centre, who published *A Stone's Throw from Embankment*, a collection written during that residency. In 1998 he was writer-in-residence for the BBC with the Windrush project, and Bard at the Beeb, a selection of poems written during that residency, was published by BBC Learning Support. He was writer in residence at the National Maritime Museum in Greenwich in 2007.

He has also written plays. He lives with the poet Grace Nichols and family in Sussex, and they received the CLPE Poetry Award 2003 for *Under the Moon and Over the Sea* (Walker Books), a children's anthology they co-edited.